BRITISH RAILWAYS

PAST and PRESENT

No 27

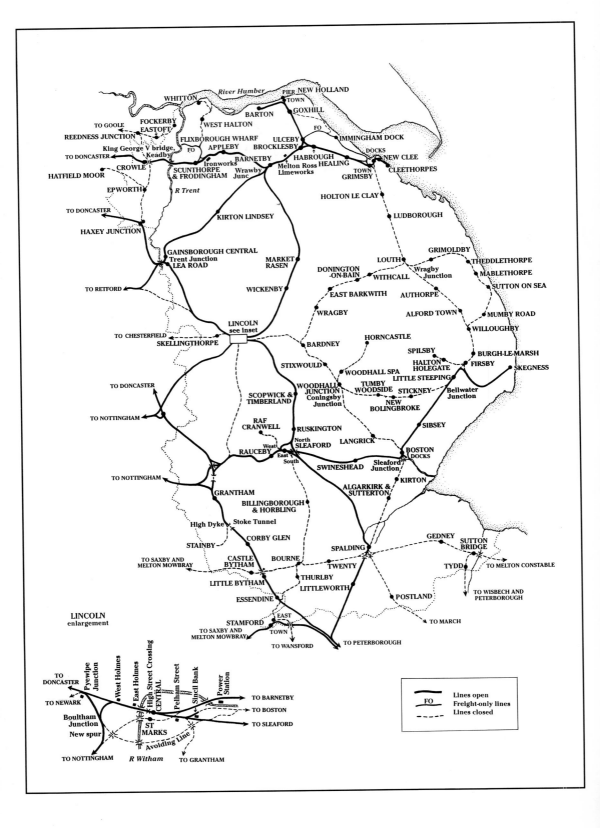

BRITISH RAILWAYS

PAST and PRESENT

No 27

Lincolnshire

Roger Hill & Carey Vessey

Past and Present

Past & Present Publishing Ltd

To Jade, Autumn, Alexandra and Victoria

First published in January 1996
Reprinted May 1997
Reprinted December 1999

British Library Cataloguing in Publication Data

A catalogue record for this book is available from the British Library

ISBN 1 85895 083 X

Past & Present Publishing Ltd
The Trundle
Ringstead Road
Great Addington
Kettering
Northants
NN14 4BW

Tel/Fax 01536 330588
email sales@slinkp-p.demon.co.uk

Printed and bound in Great Britain

HALTON HOLEGATE provides a typical scene of the rural Lincolnshire branch line. The 4½-mile branch from Firsby to Spilsby opened as an independent concern in 1868 and was taken over by the Great Northern Railway in 1891. There was one intermediate station, at Halton Holegate, seen here in November 1958, with ex-GN 'J6' 0-6-0 No 64214 heading the branch freight. Passenger services to Spilsby ceased as early as October 1939 and the line finally closed completely on 30 November 1958. The road bridge and extended station house remain in April 1995. *H. Davies/RKH*

CONTENTS

INTRODUCTION

Having already been entrusted with the East Yorkshire volume in the 'British Railways Past and Present' series (No 25), covering approximately one-third of England's largest county, we had no qualms whatsoever about tackling the 2,700 square miles or so of the second largest. Indeed, it was originally intended to cover both in one volume, but it soon became apparent that this would do justice to neither.

Many strangers to Lincolnshire describe it as 'flat and boring', but nothing could be further from the truth. From the heavy steel industry in the north to the resorts on the drier side of Britain, from highly productive farmlands to the refineries and ports in the northeast, there is much variation in the topography of the county. Before embarking on this exercise, only one of us fully appreciated this point, the other having rarely crossed the border at all. Fortunately the preparation of this book has also introduced him to the delights of places such as Lincoln and Boston, and he has even purchased a holiday caravan at Sutton on Sea.

Lincolnshire's railways suffered more than most from short-sighted mass closures between the early 1950s and 1970, completely erasing towns such as Louth, Bourne and Horncastle from the railway map and leaving vast areas of the county rail-less. Fortunately the majority of what survives is flourishing, and future closures seem in the main unlikely.

The first two sections in this book cover lines that for the most part are still open, starting with the former Great Central strongholds of the industrial north and north-east and progressing to the Lincoln area. We then move into the former Great Northern territory of the Wolds and East Lincolnshire, the majority of which has been closed for a quarter of a century. Next we look at the Boston and Sleaford areas, which, although greatly reduced in extent, still enjoy rail services, before moving further south to cover Spalding, Stamford and the popular section of the East Coast Main Line around Grantham. Readers hoping for a host of ECML pictures may well be disappointed, but we felt that these familiar locations are more than adequately covered in other works and that it would be preferable to concentrate on the lesser-known places. Even so, constraints of space have unfortunately forced us to omit some lines, such as the Torksey branch, the Lincoln-Newark and Sleaford-Spalding sections and the delightful Alford & Sutton Tramway.

As with our East Yorkshire volume, we have both derived great pleasure from compiling this book and from meeting such a host of warm and friendly people. One highlight that will not be forgotten was our day as the guests of the RAF College at Cranwell, all in response to a letter to their librarian, Mrs Buckberry, for permission to use a photograph from their archives and to visit the site to take the 'present' equivalent. We should like to express our gratitude to all the contributors of our 'past' pictures, and also to the following, without whose kind co-operation and assistance this book would not have been possible: Paul Anderson, Hugh Ballantyne, Helen Black, Bob Burdon, Peter Cook, John Foreman, Peter Grey, Alf Ludlam, John Oxley, David Perrin, Chris Prior (Loadhaul), Stewart Squires, Philip Wells, John Willerton, learned members of the RCTS, and numerous railway personnel who

LINCOLN CENTRAL: At the west end of Lincoln Central station the tracks converge into two and cross the notorious High Street level crossing. Lincoln Cathedral dominates the skyline as a filthy 'WD' 2-8-0 slams across High Street with a heavy eastbound freight in June 1964 - a picture that says it all.
  In April 1995 the author spent over two hours loitering in High Street in an effort to obtain an acceptable comparison! *C. V. Middleton/RKH*

without exception have shown great interest in what we have been seeking to achieve. Special thanks are due to John Hillier and Andrew Dibnah for their extensive help in taking 'present' pictures in the remoter corners of the county, and to Ernie Sunderland and Colin Whitfield for commendable work in the darkroom. Thanks also to Sally McKone, Lynne White and Bridget Chappell for text transcript, and last but by no means least to our long-suffering wives Jean and Lesley for their forbearance.

Roger Hill
Carey Vessey

GRIMSBY TOWN: The level crossing at the eastern end of Grimsby Town is Garden Street, seen being negotiated in the late 1950s by 'B1' No 61120 on a train for Cleethorpes. The line diverging to the right beyond the signal gantry is the former Great Northern East Lincolnshire route to Louth, Boston, Spalding and Peterborough.

Steam returned to Garden Street crossing on 20 May 1995 in the form of an excursion behind No 44767 *George Stephenson*, the first steam locomotive to visit the station for 26 years. The East Lincolnshire line closed in 1970, the Cleethorpes route is singled and the avoiding line through platform 3 behind the photographer now ends in a buffer-stop. The now-disused Garden Street box survives, and fortunately its substantial construction makes it a difficult target for vandals. *Tony Ross/RKH*

North Lincolnshire - the Great Central and branches

REEDNESS JUNCTION: The Isle of Axholme is an area in north-west Lincolnshire, so called because prior to extensive drainage works undertaken in the 17th century it was surrounded by rivers and thus isolated from the rest of the country. The Axholme Joint Railway between Marshland Junction (Goole) and Haxey Junction on the former Great Northern & Great Eastern Joint Doncaster-Gainsborough-Lincoln line was opened in 1903/4 with branches from Reedness Junction to Fockerby and from Epworth Junction to the Hatfield Moor Peat Moss Works. Until the 1923 Grouping it was operated jointly by the North Eastern and Lancashire & Yorkshire railways. Passenger services ceased in 1933 and freight finally in 1965.

Here, Goole-based LMS Class '2' 2-6-0 No 46407 stands at Reedness Junction in the late 1950s with a Goole-bound freight from the Epworth line. In the spring of 1995 the remote station house and fencing remain. *G. Oates/RKH*

EASTOFT station on the Fockerby branch on 14 September 1963, with Hunslet 0-6-0 diesel-mechanical No D2611 heading an RCTS brake-van railtour. These engines were the Goole dock shunters and were used on the branch from the end of steam until closure. Note the low platform, which was typical of the Axholme Joint stations and reflected the fact that passenger traffic was not the main reason for the line's existence. As can be seen in the corresponding June 1993 photograph, the majority of the buildings remain. *J. F. Sedgwick/RKH*

FOCKERBY: Ivatt 'Mogul' No 46407 waits to return to Goole with the daily freight on 13 August 1960, conveying an extra brake-van for a Railway Enthusiasts Club party. There were no turntables on the line and engines normally worked chimney-first from Goole.

An agricultural building now stands on the same spot, but the entrance-way from the road on the left is unaltered and behind the photographer the station house and ticket office survive. *C. H. A. Townley/RKH*

CROWLE: This delightful picture from the late 1950s shows the viaduct and swing-bridge by which the Axholme Joint crossed the former Great Central Doncaster-Scunthorpe line and the Stainforth & Keadby Canal. A Class '2' 2-6-0 heads a freight towards Goole.

The same location in May 1995 shows a Class 56 hauling a freight towards Doncaster. All that remains of the viaduct is the abutment on the southern bank. *G. Oates/RKH*

BELTON station plays host to No 46407 heading the same freight seen in the picture of Fockerby on page 11 on 13 August 1960. The platform building survives in a private garden and thanks are due to the owner for allowing access. *C. H. A. Townley/RKH*

HATFIELD MOOR: Another view taken on 13 August 1960, this time at the Peat Moss Works terminus. Although this branch closed in September 1963, peat is still an important industry in the area and the much-modernised works are shown in April 1995. The trailer on the right is standing in approximately the same spot as No 46407; note also the leaning pole in the distance just to the right of the main building, which is believed to be the same one as in the centre of the 1960 view. With thanks to Levington Horticulture Ltd for allowing access. *C. H. A. Townley/RKH*

CROSBY MINES, SCUNTHORPE: The North Lindsey Light Railway between Scunthorpe and Whitton was built by the GC and opened in 1906. Passenger services ceased in 1925, but while the northern section was finally abandoned in 1980, the southern section from Scunthorpe to Flixborough Wharf on the River Trent is still in use. This is Crosby Mines in May 1956 with former 'WD' 0-6-0STs Nos 16 and 18 of the Ore Mining Branch Scunthorpe fleet double-heading a local ironstone train on BR metals. No 16 was Hudswell Clarke No 1758 of 1943 and No 18 Bagnall No 2762 of 1944.

Crosby Mines box was burned out some years ago, but the shell survives in June 1995 as Class 60 No 60067 *James Clerk-Maxwell* heads for Flixborough Wharf with export steel from Scunthorpe. The future of the line now seems assured and it has recently been relaid and re-aligned, and re-opened to Roxby. *John Foreman/RKH*

FLIXBOROUGH WHARF in June 1956, with Peckett 0-6-0STs preparing to take imported iron ore to the John Lysaghts Ltd Normanby Park works. Lysaghts had about ten of these engines dating from between 1911 and 1918, and there were three later ones that were assembled on site from parts supplied by Pecketts.

The Wharf still operates its own fleet of diesels (including a Class 20) and the original crane survives, although dwarfed by a newer one. This spring 1993 view was taken from slightly further back than the original in order to show the rail connection. *John Foreman/RKH*

WEST HALTON was on the northern section of the North Lindsey line, and is seen here with ex-GC 'J11' 0-6-0 No 64419 heading an RCTS railtour on 20 June 1954. Note the smart fashions of the day - jackets and ties for the men, dresses for the ladies and not a pair of jeans, an anorak or a duffel-bag in sight! Can any readers identify themselves?

The only trace of the railway at this location today is the remains of the station yard gate, and for this reason the June 1995 view has been taken from slightly further back than the original. *W. Woolhouse/RKH*

KING GEORGE V BRIDGE, KEADBY: The former Great Central Doncaster-Scunthorpe line and the main A18 road share the King George V Bridge across the River Trent at Keadby, opened in 1916. The eastern end of the bridge was designed to lift for the passage of river traffic, but this facility ceased in 1956. In May of that year ex-works GC 'O4/3' 2-8-0 No 63696 heads an eastbound freight as an Austin Ruby trundles along an otherwise deserted A18. The lifting end of the bridge is on the left.

Class 60 No 60026 *William Caxton* at the same location on 20 May 1995. Apart from the increased headroom for road traffic and the provision of a separate footpath, the bridge has changed little, and despite appearances the A18 is an incredibly busy road. The positioning of the lone car was a sheer fluke. *John Foreman/RKH*

GUNHOUSE BANK, SCUNTHORPE: The pioneer 'B1' 4-6-0, No 61000 *Springbok*, heads a Doncaster-Scunthorpe freight up the 1 in 93 of Gunhouse bank at the western approach to Scunthorpe on 21 April 1960, banked by the usual tender-first 'O4'. By this time *Springbok* had been displaced from her native East Anglia by diesels and transferred to Doncaster.

In May 1995 Class 60 No 60068 *Charles Darwin* heads an empty MGR train past the same spot. Considerable tree-felling has been undertaken in order to combat wheel slippage. *John Foreman/CV*

SCUNTHORPE & FRODINGHAM (1): At the western end of the station in 1960 No 63696 is acting as the Gunhouse banker, waiting to return to the foot of the bank to resume her duties.

In May 1995 a Cleethorpes-Manchester Class 158 'Sprinter' calls at the station. The footbridge has been replaced and the through tracks behind the station reduced to two, with the remainder of the extensive yard area lying mostly derelict. The short bay in which the 'O4' was standing can still be identified, although now devoid of track. *J. F. Oxley/CV*

SCUNTHORPE & FRODINGHAM (2): Cambridge-based 'B1' No 61300, running-in after overhaul at Doncaster Works, heads east through Scunthorpe & Frodingham with a Doncaster-Cleethorpes excursion on 18 June 1961. The view from the same footbridge in May 1995 sees a Manchester-Cleethorpes Class 158 leaving the station and heading for Barnetby. *John Foreman/CV*

FRODINGHAM YARD (1): Ex-North Eastern 'B16/1' 4-6-0 No 61416 passes Frodingham Yard No 1 signal box in June 1956 with the 8.15 pm Frodingham (Trent Yard)-York freight, a regular 'B16' working at the time. Frodingham Ironworks dominate the background.

In May 1995 Class 56 No 56051 *Isle of Grain* passes the site of the box with loaded steel. The Class 37 just visible on the extreme left is employed trip-shunting coal to the steelworks. Note how the modernisation of the works has altered the skyline. *John Foreman/CV*

FRODINGHAM YARD (2): 'O4/1' 2-8-0 No 63586 works No 10 Pilot out of 'Entrance E' sidings towards Frodingham West Yard with mineral empties in October 1964. This duty was mostly assigned to elderly 'O4s' from Frodingham shed, one of which (No 63601) is preserved as part of the National Collection. This branch and sidings were brought into use during 1939 when the first of the Appleby-Frodingham blast furnaces known as the 'Queens' was commissioned.

By March 1995 the sidings have been abandoned, but the 'Queens' still dominate the Scunthorpe skyline.
John Foreman/RKH

FRODINGHAM MPD (coded 36C by BR) is seen in late 1964 with 'WD' 2-8-0 No 90032 receiving attention, and 'O4' No 63586 and 'K1' 2-6-0 No 62015 peering out of the gloom.

The steam shed was closed in February 1966 and demolished, and a diesel depot was built slightly to the west of the site. This is now used for storing withdrawn locomotives such as Class 47s Nos 47413/18/06, seen here in early 1995. *John Foreman/RKH*

APPLEBY (LINCS) was photographed in June 1956 with 'O2/3' 2-8-0 No 63948 piloting an 'O4/8' hammering up the 1 in 96 climb out of the Ancholme Valley on the eastern approach to Scunthorpe from Barnetby with a train of empty steel plate wagons from Annesley.

Somewhat surprisingly, the GC signal box survives and the level crossing gates on this busy line are still operated by handwheel mechanism installed by the LNER during the Second World War. The view of the location in the summer of 1993 shows Class 56 No 56116 rumbling past light engine. *John Foreman/CV*

BARNETBY (1): This view looking west towards Wrawby Junction from Barnetby station in the 1950s shows a Gresley 'J39' 0-6-0 passing with an eastbound freight. Three former GC lines converge at Wrawby Junction, from Scunthorpe, Gainsborough and Lincoln, all opened in 1848/49.

Apart from the Gainsborough line, which now only carries a Saturday service of three passenger trains in each direction per week, Barnetby is still a thriving station and, with the exception of the East Coast Main Line, the section east to Brocklesby is probably the busiest stretch of railway in Lincolnshire. Apart from a frequent passenger service, it carries all freight into and out of Immingham and, although the semaphore signalling has been much reduced, Wrawby Junction is believed to be the second largest manual signal box still in use in the country, next to Shrewsbury Severn Bridge. Class 60 No 60024 *Elizabeth Fry* rumbles through the station with iron ore empties for Immingham in March 1995. *Scunthorpe Evening Telegraph/RKH*

BARNETBY (2): At the eastern end of Barnetby, looking from the station footbridge on 3 August 1959, a Derby Heavyweight DMU arrives forming a New Holland-Lincoln service.

Apart from the refurbishment of Barnetby East box and the abandonment of the cattle dock, little has changed in March 1995 as Class 60 No 60014 *Alexander Fleming* passes with iron ore for Scunthorpe, imported through Immingham. *J. Spencer Gilks/CV*

MELTON ROSS LIMEWORKS: During a period of track relaying in June 1963 a 'WD' creeps slowly eastwards towards the exchange sidings with Melton Ross Limeworks, midway between Barnetby and Brocklesby. Note the rail connection to the works on the left, which at that time provided virtually all the limestone requirements for Scunthorpe's steel-making.

The same view from the A18 road bridge in May 1995 sees Class 60 No 60008 *Moel Fammau* approaching with an Immingham-Scunthorpe iron ore train. Lorry-loads of limestone now clog up the already overcrowded roads and the up slow line has been severed, although the extreme right-hand line in this view was re-instated during March 1995 after several years of two-track working between Brocklesby Junction and Barnetby. *John Foreman/RKH*

BROCKLESBY is at the western apex of a triangle linking lines to Ulceby (for Immingham) to the north and Habrough (for Grimsby and Cleethorpes) to the east. 'O4/7' 2-8-0 No 63634 heads a Grimsby-bound coal train through the station in about 1957.

Although the station is now closed, the attractive listed 1840s buildings (which are reputed to have been designed to the specification of the Earl of Yarborough to impress important visitors to his nearby estate) and the unusual low-level signal box with the mechanism below the platform, survive virtually unaltered 38 years on as Class 37 No 37344 passes with an Immingham-bound empty TEA oil tank train in June 1995. *Tony Ross/Andrew Dibnah*

BARTON-ON-HUMBER is the terminus of a 9-mile branch from Ulceby via New Holland, built by the Manchester, Sheffield & Lincolnshire Railway (later the GCR) and opened in 1848/49. On 11 October 1964 a Derby DMU awaits departure for Cleethorpes.

While its infrastructure has declined over the last 30 years, the branch is still busy and Barton is the interchange for a regular bus service over the Humber Bridge to Hull. Here is the station in May 1993 with a Class 153 single unit about to fill up and leave for Cleethorpes. *T. J. Edgington/CV*

NEW HOLLAND PIER: *Above* For 150 years prior to the opening of the Humber Bridge in 1981 the Humber was crossed by ferries, initially from Barton, but after 1848 from the 1,500-foot rail-connected wooden pier at New Holland. In this evocative picture dating from August 1962 'Britannia' 'Pacific' No 70041 *Sir John Moore* awaits departure for Cleethorpes alongside the LNER-built paddle-steamers *Lincoln Castle* (1940) nearest the camera and either *Wingfield Castle* or *Tattershall Castle* (1934) behind.

Right The ferry crossing, which was operated by BR and its predecessors, could take anything from 20 minutes to in excess of 2 hours, depending upon the wind, tide and notorious Humber shifting sands, whereas today it takes no more than 2 or 3 minutes to cross the bridge by road. In 1983 the pier was taken over as it stood by New Holland Bulk Services Ltd who, apart from removing the signals and the northern section of the down track, left the platform, buildings and signal box intact and installed conveyors and ship-loading gantries to move grain and other freight. The roof of the signal box (which still contains the levers) and the platform awnings can still be seen behind the conveyor in the July 1994 view; thanks are due to the company for allowing access. *B. Todd/CV*

Right Another view of the pier looking north on 3 June 1952 with ex-GN 'K2' 2-6-0 No 61730 ready to depart with the 5.07 pm to Cleethorpes. *T. J. Edgington*

NEW HOLLAND TOWN (1): Immediately to the south of the pier was New Holland Town station, which formed the northern apex of a triangle with the lines to Ulceby and Cleethorpes to the south and Barton to the west. The same train as that seen on the previous page draws off the pier into the station behind *Sir John Moore*.

Town station was demolished by New Holland Bulk Services and the site is now occupied by their depot and huge grain silos. A small section of railway was retained and some new sidings constructed, although these are rarely used today. The company operates its own Sentinel 0-6-0 diesel shunter, seen in this July 1994 picture. Note under the conveyor the track on which the 'Britannia' is running, and the same point where the wooden decking of the pier changes to terra firma. *B. Todd/RKH*

NEW HOLLAND TOWN (2): The view south from the footbridge in June 1961 shows a Derby Heavyweight DMU departing for Cleethorpes, as well as the extensive sidings and part of the triangular track layout referred to opposite. The Heavyweights were part of the Lincolnshire scene for more than 35 years.

In the 1995 view from the New Holland Bulk Services yard, Barrow Road signal box and the Lincoln Castle (formerly the Yarborough) Hotel stand out as a Barton-Cleethorpes Class 153 negotiates the west-to-south curve of the former triangle. A single wooden platform and 'bus shelter' now serves as New Holland station just to the south of Barrow Road box. *B. Todd/CV*

ULCEBY on 22 August 1963 with 'Britannia' No 70037 *Hereward the Wake*, uncommonly grimy for an Immingham passenger engine, working a New Holland-Cleethorpes local.

Ulceby station is still open and the massive wooden GC South Junction signal box survives in a much patched-up condition to control the junctions of the lines to Immingham, New Holland and Brocklesby. A Cleethorpes-bound Class 153 departs in March 1995. *D. P. Leckonby/CV*

HABROUGH station is at the eastern apex of the Ulceby triangle. In June 1959 DMUs bound respectively for Cleethorpes and probably Lincoln pass at the staggered platforms flanking the level crossing.

Little has changed at Habrough by June 1995 as a Cleethorpes-Sheffield Class 158 approaches the up platform. For such a relatively small place, Habrough enjoys an intensive rail service with more than 30 trains in each direction on weekdays. *J. F. Oxley/RKH*

HEALING is two stations on from Habrough towards Grimsby, and on 18 June 1961 a Castleford-Cleethorpes excursion passes behind LMS 2-6-0 No 42963; this must have been an extremely rare entry in the local spotters' notebooks.

Virtually all traffic on the Grimsby line today consists of 'Sprinters', and as with most other seaside resorts, rail excursions to Cleethorpes are rare indeed. A Barton-Cleethorpes Class 153 slows for its stop on 27 June 1995. *John Willerton/RKH*

LITTLEFIELD LANE CROSSING, GRIMSBY: Heading west out of Grimsby past Littlefield Lane crossing on 17 June 1961 is 'B1' No 61225 with an evening stopping train.

On 20 May 1995 preserved LMS 'Black Five' 4-6-0 No 44767 *George Stephenson* became the first steam locomotive to visit Grimsby for 26 years, and John Willerton returned to Littlefield Lane to repeat his 'past' picture. The crossing has now been automated and although the box still stands it has been heavily vandalised. *Both John Willerton*

FRIARGATE CROSSING, GRIMSBY, is the first crossing out of Grimsby Town station to the west, and on 3 August 1958 ex-GC 'Director' 4-4-0 No 62662 *Prince of Wales* heads a Sheffield-Cleethorpes excursion. The 'Directors' were frequently seen on this work at the time, but within two years, apart from the preserved *Butler-Henderson*, they had all gone for scrap.

In the second view a Manchester-Cleethorpes Class 156 'Sprinter' passes the same location on 27 June 1995. *John Willerton/RKH*

GRIMSBY TOWN (I): A typically grimy 'WD', No 90425, clanks into Grimsby Town from the west with a stone train in about 1957. The authors advise the reader to pause for a minute and study the wealth of detail in this superb picture, especially the vintage car visible through the fencing on the left and the spotter on the wall at the extreme right, busily making up his notebook.

On 27 June 1995 a Manchester-Cleethorpes Class 158 passes the same spot. The modern signalling is now controlled from Pasture Street box, Wellowgate box has gone and there is nothing left to interest the local spotters. Little else, however, has changed and the cramped station still suffers from having a busy level crossing at either end of it. *Tony Ross/RKH*

GRIMSBY TOWN (2): The GC station at Grimsby Town was opened in 1848 and, being a principal station, was given an overall roof. Here is the view looking west from Garden Street on 10 September 1960 as 'K3' 2-6-0 No 61981 heads through platform 1 with Woodford Halse-Grimsby Docks fish empties, and 'B1' No 61074 waits in platform 2 with the 12.30 to Peterborough.

The overall roof has been renewed and the track layout much simplified, but St James's parish church and the Yarborough Hotel still dominate the background. In July 1995 a Manchester-Cleethorpes Class 158 stands at platform 1, and a Class 153 forming a Lincoln service at the truncated platform 3. *Roger Hockney/RKH*

GRIMSBY DOCKS: The Great Central opened the branch from Grimsby Town to Grimsby Docks station in 1853, and ten years later extended it to Cleethorpes. On 7 August 1963 LMS 'Crab' 2-6-0 No 42897 passes Grimsby Docks station with empty stock for New Clee Sidings. A vintage 'blood and custard' BR Advertising Unit Austin van on the right and the photographer's bike on the left complete the scene.

The footbridge from which the 'past' picture was taken has been demolished, but a similar view is obtainable in July 1995 from the Cleethorpes Road flyover. The station is still open and a Manchester-bound Class 158 passes the remaining platform. The Spillers building is still prominent on the right horizon. *Roger Hockney/RKH*

NEW CLEE SIDINGS (1): On a typical summer Saturday or Bank Holiday in the late 1950s, as many as 40 excursion trains would arrive at Cleethorpes and plenty of storage capacity was essential. This is New Clee Sidings on 28 June 1959 with, from left to right, the following excursions ready to back down into Cleethorpes station to pick up their returning passengers: 'B1s' Nos 61165, 61377 and 61230, bound respectively for Rotherham, Doncaster and Fitzwilliam; 'Director' No 62668 *Jutland* for Sutton-in-Ashfield; 'K3' No 61824 for Sheffield; 'B1s' Nos 61208 and 61231 for Worksop; 'K3' No 61803 for Harworth Colliery; and finally the celebrated *Butler-Henderson* will return to Kirkby-in-Ashfield.

The 1995 picture speaks for itself as a Class 153 heads for Cleethorpes along the remaining single line. The floodlights belong to Grimsby Town Football Club. *N. E. Stead/CV*

NEW CLEE SIDINGS (2): We are now looking west from the footbridge at Fuller Street on 16 September 1959 as Carlisle (Kingmoor) 'Black Five' No 44792 brings in another excursion.

Nearly 36 years later a unique opportunity arose to repeat this picture with No 44767, also an ex-Kingmoor engine. Again, further commentary on the background is unnecessary, save to point out the distinctive tower on the horizon. *Both John Willerton*

CLEETHORPES on 28 July 1979 is host to 'Deltic' No 55021 *Argyll & Sutherland Highlander* shunting the stock of a King's Cross through train.

The through service to London ceased in 1993, and in May 1995 the author had to be content with the inevitable 'Sprinter' arriving from Manchester. The track layout has been much simplified and the semaphore signalling removed, and as will be seen from the cover picture, the station itself now seems far less important. *G. W. Morrison/RKH*

Opposite page ADMIRALTY PLATFORM HALT, IMMINGHAM: By the early years of the century the port of Grimsby was outgrowing its capacity and expansion elsewhere was essential. Nearby Immingham was ideal, possessing a deep water channel and cheap land, and the Great Central Railway's dock there was duly opened by King George V in 1912. In addition to Grimsby, there were rail connections to Ulceby in the west and to Goxhill on the New Holland line to the north. Admiralty Platform Halt on the Goxhill line was built for the use of workers at the nearby petro-chemical works and a Derby DMU forming an enthusiasts special is seen there on 7 October 1967.

Although the track to the south of the Halt still remains, it has not been used for several years and has been lifted north to Goxhill. Here is the view showing the redundant track in May 1995. *T. J. Edgington/RKH*

IMMINGHAM DOCK: The windswept Immingham Dock station was the terminus of the passenger services from Ulceby and Goxhill, which finally expired in 1969. On 3 June 1952 ex-GC 'A5' 'Pacific' tank No 69820 waits to leave with the 2.45 pm to New Holland.

The station site in May 1993 is overshadowed by a Panamanian-registered cargo vessel clearing the lock on the way out of the dock into the Humber. It is truly amazing that right in the middle of one of the most modern deep-water ports in Europe there can still be found a row of leaning telegraph poles dating from another generation. *T. J. Edgington/CV*

IMMINGHAM MPD (coded 40B by BR) was opened in 1913 and closed to steam in February 1966. This is the western end of the main shed building on 7 November 1962. The identifiable 'B1' is No 61314 and the 'Britannia' on the right is believed to be No 70039 *Sir Christopher Wren*. For the record, there were 64 steam locomotives and just six diesel shunters on shed that day, including all of Immingham's allocation of seven 'Britannias' except No 70037.

The present-day shot, dated 25 September 1995, was the last to be taken for this book, and shows the typical motive power allocated to the depot. Although some of the buildings in the original photograph have been removed, the remainder still stand, albeit with renewed cladding. Belonging to Loadhaul, the depot's modern facilities on the site of an old steam shed seem quite incongruous. *Ken Fairey/CV*

GRIMSBY & IMMINGHAM ELECTRIC TRAMWAY (1): No book including the railways of Grimsby and Immingham would be complete without coverage of the Grimsby & Immingham Electric Tramway, opened by the GCR in 1912 and finally closed by BR on 1 July 1961. Here is the depot at Pyewipe after the very last journey on that day. Cars Nos 1, 4 and 12 are part of the original GC batch of 1912 and Nos 18 and 27 are two of the 20 cars purchased from Gateshead between 1948 and 1951.

The disused depot building still stands in May 1995. Note on the extreme left one of the metal poles embedded in a block of concrete, which has simply been uprooted and abandoned. *Hugh Ballantyne/RKH*

GRIMSBY & IMMINGHAM ELECTRIC TRAMWAY (2): In 1956 the street portion of the tramway in Grimsby was closed and the eastern terminus cut back to Cleveland Bridge. Two of the original GC cars wait here in June 1959, alongside the main reason for the demise of the tramway.
    At the same location in May 1995, the road is ironically closed to traffic. *J. F. Oxley/RKH*

GRIMSBY & IMMINGHAM ELECTRIC TRAMWAY (3): Two more ex-GC cars stand at the Tramway Station terminus at Corporation Bridge in Grimsby in the early 1950s. The Spillers building still dominates the background at this location in May 1995. *H. Davies/CV*

KIRTON LINDSEY on the former GC Gainsborough-Barnetby line on a gloomy 7 March 1977, with Class 47 No 47218 heading an MGR train of coal bound for export through Immingham.

As mentioned earlier, this line now only carries trains of any description on Saturdays and surely cannot survive for much longer. On 1 July 1995 the last train for a week, the 1802 from Cleethorpes, leaves for Gainsborough Central, Retford and Sheffield. *G. B. Wise/RKH*

GAINSBOROUGH TRENT JUNCTION: The former GC signal box was photographed on Christmas Eve 1962 with a 'WD'-hauled freight signalled for Gainsborough Central and the Barnetby line. The other signals refer to the former Great Northern & Great Eastern Joint line to Gainsborough Lea Road and Lincoln.

The GC box has since been demolished and replaced by a modern structure behind the photographer in this June 1995 view of a 'Sprinter' taking the Lea Road line to form a service to Lincoln. *Mike Black/RKH*

GAINSBOROUGH LEA ROAD (1) on 31 August 1963 with York-based 'B1' No 61031 *Reedbuck* heading the 4.37 pm (Saturdays only) York-Yarmouth train.

A Doncaster-Peterborough 'Sprinter' arrives at Lea Road in June 1995. The goods shed has been demolished but, in contrast to Gainsborough Central, Lea Road remains a busy and attractive station on which a great deal of money has been spent in recent years. *D. P. Leckonby/Andrew Dibnah*

GAINSBOROUGH LEA ROAD (2): The platforms at Lea Road are staggered, and on Christmas Eve 1962 BR '9F' 2-10-0 No 92144 passes the delightful GN-style signal box at the south end of the up platform with a freight.

In June 1995 a Class 153 bound for Peterborough passes the box, which happily is as tidy as 33 years before, although it has lost one of its GN-pattern bargeboards. *Mike Black/RKH*

The Lincoln area

LINCOLN CENTRAL (1): The magnificent Great Northern Railway station at Lincoln Central was opened in 1850, and here is the classic view of all eight platforms from Pelham Street flyover on 30 August 1958. On the left an ex-GE 'J69' 0-6-0T with a vintage coach acts as yard pilot, Rolls Royce-engined Cravens and Derby Heavyweight DMUs are respectively in platforms 8 and 6, 'K2' No 61746 blows off in the centre road and another Heavyweight leaves platform 4 forming a service for Boston via Woodhall Junction.

In May 1995 a Class 153 leaves for Sleaford. Despite a considerable amount of rationalisation and the abandonment of platforms 1, 2 and 8, Lincoln Central remains one of the most attractive stations in the country, with full semaphore signalling and much more to interest the railway historian. *John Foreman/RKH*

LINCOLN CENTRAL (2): In the first 'past' picture, dated 20 May 1949, 'B16/3' No 61448 leaves platform 6 with a Yarmouth-York express and approaches High Street level crossing at the west end of the station.

A multi-storey car park now dominates the scene beyond the crossing, as seen in the April 1995 view of a Class 153 departing for Newark. The bracket signals are only a few feet away from the crossing and seem rather out of place in the middle of a bustling modern city. *P. H. Wells/RKH*

In the third intermediate picture from 21 March 1973, a two-car Heavyweight DMU forming the 1455 from Sheffield passes High Street box and enters Platform 5. This picture is particularly interesting since it shows the view after the demolition of the old buildings to the north of High Street crossing but before the construction of the car park. *G. B. Wise*

LINCOLN ST MARKS (1): On 16 May 1954 at the former Midland Railway St Marks station, LMS Compound 4-4-0 No 41181 waits to depart with the 8.00 pm mail to Tamworth.

St Marks closed on 11 May 1985 when a short length of new line was opened, enabling the diversion of all traffic into the renovated Central station. Unfortunately, although the frontage is a listed structure, the interior was simply left to rot and the second picture is the view in March 1995, showing the main station buildings on the left and, immediately below the building centre right, the remains of the platform at which the Compound was standing.

The third picture shows the trackbed, parts of which were excavated to a great depth by archaeologists uncovering an 8th-century Carmelite Friary. *J. F. Oxley/RKH/CV*

LINCOLN ST MARKS (2): BR Class '4' 4-6-0 No 75055 approaches St Marks from the west with a coal train for Immingham on 27 May 1961. Note the small two-road shed on the left, which had closed two years earlier. The second picture shows the view of the devastation from the remains of the platform in March 1995. *J. F. Oxley/RKH*

EAST HOLMES (I): Perhaps the best-known of all Lincoln's railway views is the superb Cathedral-dominated setting of Brayford Pool. Here is the scene in about 1957 with ex-GN 'J6' 0-6-0 No 64260 heading east towards Central with a brake-van. Will the young fisherman see this book and recognise himself today?

The inevitable Class 153 crosses the low bridge in March 1995. The City Flour Mills and British Railways Wet Bond Store have been replaced by modern office blocks, but essentially the scene is unchanged. *Tony Ross/RKH*

EAST HOLMES (2): Engineering works on the East Coast Main Line regularly led to the diversion of traffic through Lincoln, and on 28 September 1958 'A3' 'Pacific' No 60071 *Tranquil* passes the ex-GN shed (coded 40A by BR) with a northbound diversion. The roof of East Holmes box can be seen above the second coach.

The shed closed in January 1964, but amazingly, more than 30 years later, the buildings survive virtually intact. In March 1995 a Class 153 from Gainsborough heads towards Central past East Holmes box, yet another pure Great Northern survivor. *N. E. W. Skinner/RKH*

PELHAM STREET (1): The Pelham Street flyover afforded not only an excellent view of Lincoln Central but also of eastbound trains leaving St Marks. On 12 May 1979 'Deltic' No 55009 *Alycidon* heads the 1304 King's Cross-Cleethorpes towards the flat crossing seen overleaf.

The track at this point was lifted and the footbridge removed following the closure of St Marks, but several of the background buildings remain in March 1995. *G. W. Morrison/CV*

PELHAM STREET (2): The line from St Marks crossed the Lincoln Central-Sleaford line on a flat crossing before connecting with the spur from Central on to the former GC line to Market Rasen and Barnetby. On 28 July 1979 a Heavyweight DMU comes off Lincoln diesel depot and heads across the Midland tracks into Central past Pelham Street box. The box in the top centre is Sincil Bank, which formerly controlled the junctions with the ex-GN lines to Boston and Grantham.

The flat crossing was removed following the closure of St Marks and Sincil Bank crossing has been automated, but Pelham Street box is still operational. In April 1995 light Class 37 No 37717 moves out of Central and heads towards Market Rasen. *G. W. Morrison/RKH*

WEST HOLMES box controlled an extensive goods yard to the west of Central as well as the main line to Gainsborough and Doncaster and the spur from Boultham Junction on the Lincoln Avoiding Line. On 26 July 1958 'A4' 'Pacific' No 60015 *Quicksilver* heads away from Central past the box with a northbound diverted East Coast express.

The same view from the signal box balcony in June 1995 shows a Newark-bound Class 153. The goods yard has greatly contracted but the Boultham Junction spur remains in use by traffic bound for Newark and Nottingham. *G. Flatters/CV*

ST SWITHIN'S POWER STATION: On 3 June 1950 'O2/3' No 63960 heads a freight north out of Lincoln on the former GC line towards Market Rasen and Barnetby, crossing the River Witham at Stamp End past St Swithin's Power Station.

Yet another Class 153, bound for Grimsby, is seen at the same location in June 1995. Although the main building remains, the Power Station is now disused. *Ralph Bates (courtesy P. Grey)/CV*

LINCOLN AVOIDING LINE: The 3-mile Lincoln Avoiding Line ran to the south of the city and was opened in 1882 to enable through traffic to bypass the already congested central routes. On 2 March 1957 'K1' No 62018 heads a westbound train of coal empties from March past the public field known locally as Cow Paddle and across the former GN line from Grantham.

The Grantham line closed in 1965 and the Avoiding Line itself in 1982. The remains of the embankment and the distinctive raised footpath identify the location in April 1995. *R. E. Burdon/RKH*

WICKENBY: Ex-LMS '4F' 0-6-0 No 44394 stands in Wickenby station on the former GC Lincoln-Market Rasen-Barnetby line in March 1960. Although the station is long closed and demolished, the station house, the smart GC box and the hand-operated crossing gates remain in July 1995. *Mike Black/RKH*

MARKET RASEN is seen on 17 March 1963 with a Lincoln-bound Cravens DMU arriving. Market Rasen is now the only intermediate station open between Lincoln and Barnetby and, apart from the removal of the water tower, crane and siding, virtually nothing has changed in more than 30 years as a Grimsby-Lincoln Class 158 arrives in June 1995. *Mike Black/CV*

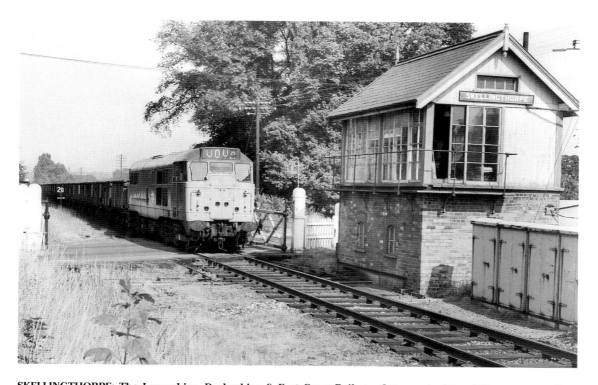

SKELLINGTHORPE: The Lancashire, Derbyshire & East Coast Railway (later part of the GC) was a grandiose scheme that never actually reached Lancashire or the East Coast, but eventually contented itself with a 58-mile length between Chesterfield and Pyewipe Junction, to the west of Lincoln Central. Regular passenger traffic ceased in 1955 and freight in 1980. On 22 July 1976 Class 31 No 31281 heads west past Skellingthorpe with Frodingham (Scunthorpe)-Mansfield coal empties.

The signal box was demolished in 1985 and its concrete base and the overgrown trackbed are all that remain in June 1995. *P. Grey/CV*

SCOPWICK & TIMBERLAND is one of the closed stations on the former GN&GE Joint line between Lincoln and Sleaford; in December 1962 '9F' No 92199 heads a southbound freight.

The attractive box and vintage crossing gates remain in July 1995. Freight services on this line are extinct, and it was decided to include this picture rather than yet another Class 153, which is the only form of traction now on offer. *Mike Black/RKH*

RUSKINGTON: Class 31 No 31103 heads a northbound mixed freight past the old closed station at Ruskington on the Lincoln-Sleaford line on 12 August 1974.

Happily the passenger service on the GN&GE Joint is flourishing, and with local authority support a new station was opened at Ruskington in 1975. Twenty years later the station is still well patronised and enjoys a weekday service of 14 southbound and 13 northbound trains. The 1505 Peterborough-Lincoln calls on 1 July 1995. *G. B. Wise/RKH*

The Wolds

BARDNEY was, as the sign proclaims, the junction on the former GN Lincoln-Boston line for the branch across the Wolds to Wragby and Louth. On 13 October 1951 'J11' No 64320 arrives with the branch pick-up freight.

The Louth branch closed completely by 1960 and the Lincoln-Boston line as a through route in 1970, although a freight facility as far as Bardney continued until 1983 for the benefit of the adjoining British Sugar Corporation works. All that remains in April 1995 is the background factory building and former goods depot awning. *P. H. Wells/RKH*

WRAGBY: Passenger services on the Bardney-Louth branch ceased in November 1951, and by the time this picture of 'J6' No 64219 was taken in October 1959 Wragby had become the railhead served by one daily freight from Lincoln; this service also perished a year later.

Virtually all the stations on the branch survive today, and here is Wragby in May 1995. The station house is now owned by Mr & Mrs I. Swallow, who kindly allowed access. *Mike Black/RKH*

EAST BARKWITH: Ex-GN 'C12' 'Atlantic' tank No 67379 heads a branch train towards Louth on 13 October 1951. These graceful engines operated on the line for more than 30 years; No 67379 was allocated to Louth for the whole of that time and worked the very last passenger train on 3 November 1951.

 The single platform, loading dock, station house and distinctive row of trees remain in March 1995. *P. H. Wells/RKH*

DONINGTON-ON-BAIN (1): Track recovery in progress at the station on 26 February 1960 contrasts with the March 1995 view from the same road overbridge showing the attractively restored station buildings. *J. F. Oxley/RKH*

DONINGTON-ON-BAIN (2): Six years earlier, on 16 May 1954, 'J6' No 64199 headed the RCTS Lincolnshire rail-tour, visiting Bardney, Louth, Willoughby (via Mablethorpe), Firsby, Spilsby, Woodhall Junction and Horncastle. Here the train pauses for photographs at Donington-on-Bain.

By March 1993 the road bridge (the same one from which the previous pictures were taken) had been filled in and the trackbed returned to agriculture. *Hugh Ballantyne/RKH*

WITHCALL: 'C12' No 67384 arrives at Withcall with the 9.55 am Bardney-Louth service on 10 April 1951. Forty-four years later, in May 1995, the platform edging survives and includes in places inset bricks bearing the manufacturer's name and date. *Mike Black/RKH*

STIXWOULD was south of Bardney on the Lincoln-Boston line, and this August 1970 photograph records a call by a Cravens DMU bound for Lincoln and Sheffield.

The two present pictures at this remote location were taken in May 1995 and show the surviving crossing gates and platforms and the station house, into which the owner has ingeniously incorporated the signal box as a sun-lounge.
P. Grey/RKH (2)

WOODHALL SPA: The 7½-mile branch from Woodhall Junction to Horncastle opened in 1855. There was one intermediate station, at Woodhall Spa, and on 24 September 1952 the 4.05 pm from Horncastle calls there, headed by ex-GC 'N5' 0-6-2T No 69275. The train consists of a vintage ex-GN articulated saloon, built in 1905 and originally part of steam railcar stock, which worked on the branch for many years.

The branch passenger service ceased as early as 1954, although freight lingered until 1971. The station site is now a car park and the trackbed to Horncastle has been converted into a public footpath. Woodhall Spa is an attractive town and well worth a visit. *J. F. Oxley/RKH*

WOODHALL JUNCTION was the junction for the Horncastle branch. On 22 April 1953 'J6' No 64180 ambles towards the junction along the bank of the River Witham with a pick-up freight from Lincoln. Enthusiasts who today seek to recreate branch freights on preserved lines should study this delightful picture carefully.

The exact location of John Oxley's picture cannot be precisely identified today, but John's own remarkable memory led the author to this spot, where the trees certainly bear a similarity to the originals. *J. F. Oxley/RKH*

HORNCASTLE terminus on 14 March 1952, with No 69275 again arriving from Woodhall Junction. The station buildings were not demolished until 1985 and the site today is partly occupied by a haulage contractor, while the remainder is a derelict wasteland. The sole surviving remnant of the railway is the southern end of the main platform, which is seen from beneath a couple of rusty trailers in April 1995. *J. F. Oxley/RKH*

TUMBY WOODSIDE: The so-called 'New Line' between Coningsby Junction and Bellwater Junction to the south of Firsby was the last major line to be built in Lincolnshire and was opened by the GN in 1913. Its principal object was to provide a shorter route for coastal traffic between Lincoln, Skegness and Mablethorpe than via Boston, where a reversal was required. Five intermediate stations were provided, and here is Tumby Woodside in July 1961 with 'J11/3' No 64346 in charge of a lengthy pick-up freight. The line was double-track throughout.

In common with most of the lines in East Lincolnshire the New Line closed in October 1970, but the station house remains in April 1995, along with (behind an impenetrable jungle of undergrowth) the platforms and the eastbound buildings. *D. B. Swale/RKH*

NEW BOLINGBROKE was the next station east from Tumby Woodside, and is seen here as a Skegness-Lincoln Central Cravens DMU arrives on 16 August 1969. The remains of both platforms survive in April 1995 and the main station building is occupied by an antiques dealer. *J. Spencer Gilks/RKH*

STICKNEY station shows signs of neglect little more than a month before the New Line closed as a two-car Heavyweight DMU leaves for Firsby on 30 August 1970.

By July 1995 the road bridge has been demolished and the main A16 levelled, and the station site is occupied by a caravan sales company. Note the chimney-pot on the house just to the left of the flag, which can just be glimpsed above the right-hand cab window of the DMU in the 'past' picture. The trackbed at the other side of the road has been converted into a pleasant picnic area. *M. Hall (courtesy P. Grey)/RKH*

SPILSBY was the terminus of a 4½-mile branch from Firsby (see page 105 and the photographs of Halton Holegate on pages 4-5). The RCTS Lincolnshire railtour described on page 80 calls at Spilsby on 16 May 1954.

By June 1993 the station site was occupied by an agricultural machinery dealer and the only remaining trace of the railway is the goods shed, seen in the right background. Note the chimney on its roof apex, which can be seen protruding above the first coach in the 'past' picture. *Hugh Ballantyne/RKH*

East Lincolnshire main line and branches

The Great Northern opened its East Lincolnshire main line between Grimsby and Peterborough via Louth, Firsby, Boston and Spalding, in 1847/48, and for more than 120 years it was the main and shortest trunk route between Lincolnshire and London, before becoming by far the most notable of the October 1970 closures.

The Spalding-Peterborough section re-opened as a result of local protest in June 1971, and the Boston-Firsby South section also survives as part of the Skegness line. The 14 miles from Grimsby to Louth were singled and lingered on until December 1980 to serve the Associated British Maltsters premises at Louth.

HOLTON LE CLAY: On 25 April 1979 Class 31 No 31113 stands at the remains of Holton le Clay station with the Louth 'branch' freight. In March 1995 the trackbed and crossing gates await possible preservation (see overleaf). *M. Roughley (courtesy A. Ludlam)/RKH*

LUDBOROUGH: A 'J6' passes Ludborough with a northbound freight on 18 May 1957. In 1978 the Grimsby-Louth Railway Preservation Society was formed with the object of restoring a rail service between Grimsby and Louth, and established their headquarters at Ludborough. They have assembled a small collection of diesel locomotives and rolling-stock there and are skilfully restoring the station and signal box. Society members obligingly opened the crossing gates for the photographer and posed for the camera on 6 May 1995. *H. B. Priestley (N. Stead collection)/RKH*

LOUTH (1): A view of the station and shed yard on 8 April 1951, with a 'C12' on shed and a vintage rake of GN stock for the Mablethorpe service in the bay platform.

The closure of the freight link with Grimsby in December 1980 left Louth as the largest town in Lincolnshire without a railway. Fortunately the magnificent station building, one of the most impressive on the GN outside London, has been saved from vandals and is now listed and in the process of being converted into flats. In the view taken in the spring of 1993 the housing that now covers the remainder of the site was in the course of construction and the ABM Maltings still dominate the background. *C. H. A. Townley/RKH*

LOUTH (2): The view looking north from Louth station on 18 May 1949 with 'A5' No 69810 heading an up freight. The stock in the bay on the left would probably be used for the Grimsby local service. The comparative view in the spring of 1995 also shows the North signal box, which survives as part of the preservation scheme. *P. H. Wells/RKH*

AUTHORPE on 11 July 1959, with Immingham 'B1' No 61142 arriving with a Peterborough-Grimsby local. A southbound service stands in the staggered up platform at the other side of the level crossing. The silver-painted smokebox fittings were an Immingham trademark for a number of years.

The station house and down platform are now in private ownership and thanks are due to the owner for allowing access to the trackbed, which is now his lawn. *H. B. Priestley (A. Ludlam collection)/RKH*

ALFORD TOWN: A Heavyweight DMU enters Alford Town on 16 August 1969 forming a Grimsby-Peterborough service. Note the station building on the extreme right and the 'L'-shaped piece of stonework below the guttering. The main buildings and trackbed are now occupied by John White (Alford) Printers Ltd, to whom thanks are due for allowing access. The building referred to above is on the extreme right, and in the third picture the same distinctive piece of stonework is seen on the main inside wall of the workshop. *J. Spencer Gilks/RKH (2)*

GRIMOLDBY: The Mablethorpe Loop line left the East Lincs at Mablethorpe Junction to the south of Louth and rejoined it at Willoughby Junction, north of Firsby. On 11 July 1959 a Heavyweight DMU calls at the attractive station of Grimoldby *en route* to Mablethorpe (not, as advertised, Grimsby Town!). DMUs took over the Loop services from 1956, but they failed to save this northern section, which closed in December 1960.

The station house has been owned by Mr & Mrs B. Harland for many years, and in a remote part of their garden in April 1995 the photographer discovered the same section of platform. *H. B. Priestley (N. Stead collection)/RKH*

THEDDLETHORPE: The first station out of Mablethorpe on the northern section of the Loop was Theddlethorpe, where 'N5' No 69306 is seen leaving for Mablethorpe on 4 September 1952. The real star of this picture is the magnificent signal with its detached spectacle glasses, which presumably made life easier for the lampman.

Unfortunately the signal is long gone by March 1995, but the station house remains and the trees are actually in the process of being cleared from the trackbed. *P. H. Wells/RKH*

MABLETHORPE (1) looking north from the level crossing footbridge on 24 September 1954 as 'A5' No 69803 arrives with a Louth-Willoughby train of vintage GN stock.

    The station site is now a leisure centre, weekend market and car park. In order to achieve some elevation the author asked Mr & Mrs B. Krajnyak if he could take a picture out of the bedroom window of their home, which now occupies the trackbed immediately to the south of the site. Permission was readily granted and here is the result. *P. H. Wells/RKH*

MABLETHORPE (2): The local services on the Loop were never particularly well patronised, but in summer vast crowds of holidaymakers would travel by rail to 'Merry Mablethorpe, the Children's Playground'. As late as 1964 over three-quarters of a million people arrived in the town by train. The station was very cramped, with only single-line access at either end, and trains often had to share a platform. In this view from the summer of 1965 'B1' No 61210 has come from Nottingham and waits for a Derby DMU to depart for Willoughby in front of it.

The only feature recognisable from the car park in March 1995 is the building in the centre, visible above the roof of the nearest DMU car in the 'past' picture. The bedroom window of the house on the right is the one from which the previous 'present' picture was taken. *D. B. Swale/RKH*

SUTTON ON SEA: The southern section of the Loop from Mablethorpe to Willoughby Junction became yet another of the October 1970 casualties, and here are two 'past' views of Sutton on Sea. In the first picture, taken on the last day of service, 3 October 1970, the single-line token is handed to the driver of a Mablethorpe-Willoughby DMU.

The second view, taken on 17 May 1982, shows the remains of the station about to be demolished prior to redevelopment for housing. Note the distinctive house on the left linking these first two views, and the 'Radio Station' building on the right, which still survives in June 1995, the date of the third picture. This building was erected in the 1920s as a sewage pumping station and was used until relatively recently as offices by the local drainage and river board, but it is now disused and unfortunately is beginning to interest the vandals. *R. B. Wilkinson(2)/RKH*

MUMBY ROAD: A Willoughby-Mablethorpe service leaves Mumby Road on 10 July 1965. Note the all-wooden station, the somersault signals and the passing loop, which was generally only used in summer.

The view from the same road bridge in April 1995 shows that the station has been demolished, but the hut on the left of the station forecourt remains, along with the clump of trees in the right background. The use of a wide-angle lens also permits inclusion of part of the distinctive station house. *J. Spencer Gilks/RKH*

WILLOUGHBY is seen on 11 July 1959 with 'B1' No 61209 coming off the Mablethorpe branch with a south-bound excursion; the main line to Alford and the north is on the left. Note the lavish station gardens that over the years won many prizes for the staff.

The March 1995 view from what is now a ploughed field shows the remains of the up main platform and, on the right, the two concrete posts that once supported the station nameboard. *H. B. Priestley (A. Ludlam collection)/RKH*

BURGH-LE-MARSH on 3 August 1964, with 'B1' No 61384 approaching on an up parcels. The station and signal box survive in private ownership and thanks are due to the owners for allowing access. Until very recently, the buildings were also used in conjunction with a small railway museum housed in the former goods shed, but unfortunately this has now been closed and its contents dispersed. *J. F. Oxley/RKH*

FIRSBY (1): Here are two 'past' views of Firsby looking north, the first showing 'B1' No 61185 arriving with an up local on 18 June 1960 and the second taken a few yards further south from the down main platform on 3 December 1970, two months after complete closure. Note the ornate ironwork in the columns supporting the roof.

The goods shed survives today in the ownership of Paul Jackson Potatoes Ltd, and thanks are due to Mr Jackson for allowing access to his garden to take the present-day picture. *G. H. Brown (courtesy A. Ludlam)/R. B. Wilkinson/RKH*

FIRSBY (2): There was nowhere in Lincolnshire quite like Firsby, the junction in the middle of nowhere. It had a lavish facade and an overall roof and in its heyday saw services to Grimsby and the north; Boston, Peterborough and London; Lincoln and Sheffield via the New Line; and Skegness and the branches to Mablethorpe and Spilsby. The reader should pause for a minute and study the detail in this fine picture taken on 1 October 1953. 'J6' No 64214 (which will have had to reverse and turn on the triangle before gaining this position) heads the 1.20 pm Lincoln-Skegness train.

All that remains to identify the location in April 1995 is the former gatehouse on the left and the building down the street at the far right. *C. H. A. Townley/RKH*

FIRSBY EAST JUNCTION: Firsby station was at the northern apex of a triangle, the south-to-east leg of which was laid to an extremely tight 10-chain radius curve that enabled through traffic for Skegness from Boston and the south to avoid reversal at the station. On 6 September 1952 'K2' No 61729 takes the south curve with a Skegness-bound excursion. The east-to-north leg of the triangle curves away to the right towards Firsby station, and in the background, above the fourth and fifth coaches, can be seen the main line itself, which formed the south-to-north leg.

The south curve is still in use and in April 1995 is cautiously negotiated by a Nottingham-Skegness Class 153. The former main line formation can be seen in the background. *P. H. Wells/RKH*

SKEGNESS (1) is seen here on 12 September 1952, with 'K2' No 61762 and a 'B1' waiting to depart. Like Cleethorpes, Skegness station in 1995 is not what it was. In the mid-1950s up to 40 holiday trains would arrive every summer Saturday, and as recently as the summer of 1993 the celebrated 0812 from Leicester hauled by a pair of Class 20s would bring crowds of enthusiasts to the town. Today there are no usable carriage sidings and apart from a very occasional special, loco-hauled services are no more. The trains are now exclusively 'Sprinters', and it is rare to see more than one in the station at a time. Here an early morning service from Grantham arrives in April 1995. *P. H. Wells/RKH*

SKEGNESS (2) A panoramic view of the station exactly 12 years later, on 12 September 1964. From left to right, 'Black Five' No 44918 has arrived on the RCTS Notts and Lincs railtour, a DMU forms a local stopping service, another 'Black Five' heads a return children's outing organised by Blidworth Miners Welfare and Brush/Sulzer No D1564 (later Class 47 No 47447) and a 'B1' also await departure.

The same viewpoint in April 1995 shows a Class 156 departing for Nottingham. The GN signal box is one of the finest surviving examples, but unfortunately no somersault signals now survive anywhere on the line, the last five having been replaced in late 1995/early 1996. *D. B. Swale/RKH*

LITTLE STEEPING was the first station south of Firsby on the East Lincs, and in about 1959 a two-car Heavyweight DMU departs for Skegness. The surviving section of the East Lincs between Sibsey and the former Firsby South Junction retains its double track and gives the impression of still being an important main line. In April 1995 a Nottingham-Skegness Class 150 'Sprinter' flashes past the station house, which is all that now remains at this location.

H. B. Priestley (N. Stead collection)/RKH

Boston and Sleaford

LANGRICK was the first station out of Boston on the Lincoln line and 'K3' No 61948 is seen arriving with a Doncaster-March train in 1956. The station site is now occupied by a transport cafe and car park, but the background houses remain to identify the location. *Les Perrin/RKH*

BOSTON: The present Boston station was opened by the GN in 1850. 'J11' No 64372 heads a morning freight northwards for the East Lincs line and Grimsby in 1958.

Following removal of the canopies and through roads, the station from this angle today presents rather a barren aspect. This is a false impression for in reality it is still staffed, clean and attractive, with full facilities for passengers and even colourful gardens. A Skegness-bound Class 156 calls in June 1993. *Les Perrin/RKH*

SLEAFORD JUNCTION (1), to the south of Boston station, is seen on 22 September 1958 with '9F' No 92036 heading an up Grimsby-New England freight, signalled for the Spalding line. Busy yards abound and a 'J69' acts as pilot. The wagon works and goods offices are on the left and Broadfield Lane box can be seen in the left background. The picture was taken from the footbridge that led to Boston shed.

The contraction of Boston's railways is well portrayed in the June 1995 view. Freight services are extinct and only the single line section towards Sleaford remains, the former sidings on the right being disused. The works, offices and footbridge have gone, but Broadfield Lane box survives, although out of use, together with the concrete structure in the left foreground, the top of which can be seen at the base of the 'past' picture. A Class 156 forms a Skegness-Sleaford-Nottingham service. *John Foreman/RKH*

SLEAFORD JUNCTION (2): Looking in the opposite direction from the same footbridge on the same day, 1956-vintage Barclay 0-6-0 diesel shunter No 11186 (later D2409) and a 'J69' shunt the yards as a 'K2' stands on the up goods with a short freight. The Sleaford line curves away to the right.

The large goods shed in the centre is still in use, although no longer rail-served and several of the background buildings also survive. A Nottingham-Skegness Class 150 approaches on 18 June 1995. *John Foreman/RKH*

118

BOSTON DOCKS: Boston is a thriving port and the branch constructed in the 1880s to serve the docks remained in use until very recently. Class 08 No 08386 heads for the docks in May 1984 and passes the unique octagonal signal box and somersault signals in London Road.

The rail link to the docks is now severed, but the box, crossing and signals survive, although the left-hand somersault has been replaced with an upper quadrant arm. This delightful scene is shown to better effect in the third picture and it is hoped that action will be taken to preserve these historic structures. *Andrew Young/CV/RKH*

BOSTON SOUTH (1): An evocative picture of 'K3' No 61803 heading an evening Grimsby-King's Cross fish train past the grounds of London Road Hospital on 7 June 1953.

This location today is part of the A16 relief road. The rooftop to the right of the pair of buildings in the centre is the one seen above the right-hand buffer-beam of the 'K3'. *Les Perrin/RKH*

BOSTON SOUTH (2): Gresley 'B17/6' 4-6-0 No 61627 *Aske Hall* heads a Doncaster-March train across the bridge over the Boston South Forty Foot Drain. Note the substantial warehouse on the right, built by the GN to encourage traffic to use the railway rather than the docks.

The second picture, dating from May 1984, shows a Class 31 on what then remained of the East Lincs line south to Spalding, March and Peterborough, but with the warehouse still standing.

By June 1993 (*above*) all trace of the past has been swept away. The bridge has been renewed and the area is now part of the main A16 relief road. *Les Perrin/Andrew Young/RKH*

KIRTON: An up Heavyweight DMU passes the site of Kirton station on the last weekend of service on the East Lincs south of Boston in October 1970. The dead straight trackbed was ideal for conversion into a road, and in 1995 it duly forms part of the A16, presently as far as Algarkirk & Sutterton but with plans to extend further south towards Spalding. The roof of the goods warehouse right of centre provides the connection. *P. Grey/RKH*

SWINESHEAD station on the former GN Sleaford-Boston line opened in 1859. This view shows 'J6' No 64247 pausing with a Grantham-Boston local in June 1952.

The line from Nottingham, Grantham and Sleaford is now the only rail link with Boston from the south, and Swineshead station is still open. The 0812 Leicester-Skegness whistles through in June 1993 headed by Class 20s Nos 20128 and 20032. *Les Perrin/RKH*

SLEAFORD EAST JUNCTION on 17 August 1974, with a Cravens DMU forming the 0926 Skegness-Grantham. The train is approaching from the Boston line and the line on the embankment and bridge in the background is the former GN&GE Joint direct Sleaford Avoiding Line to Spalding. The Joint line also served Sleaford station by means of a loop diverging to the west at Sleaford North Junction and the line to the right is the spur by which this loop regained the main Joint line at Sleaford South Junction.

Despite having been singled, the layout at this location today is virtually unchanged, although since the obliteration of freight services in the area, the Avoiding Line is rarely used. A Nottingham-Skegness Class 150 heads towards Boston; note the area on the right, which is the trackbed of the former GN line to Bourne, closed completely by April 1965. *G. B. Wise/RKH*

SLEAFORD station looking west on 10 August 1974. A pair of Class 31s, Nos 31209 and 31222, are heading the summer Saturdays-only 0925 King's Cross-Skegness through train.

Today the station retains much of its character, including the awnings and footbridge, although the ornate chimney stacks have been removed. Loco-hauled and through services are no more, but this pleasant market town still enjoys a frequent service of 'Sprinters' to Boston, Skegness, Spalding, Peterborough, Lincoln and the Midlands. On 1 July 1995 a Class 153 for Lincoln leaves platform 3 on the left as a Nottingham-Skegness Class 156 approaches platform 1. *G. B. Wise/RKH*

SLEAFORD EAST: Class 47 No 47478 passes the magnificent signals to the east of Sleaford station with a return-ing Flower Festival special from Spalding on 12 May 1979.

The same location on 10 April 1993 reveals that the line into the station has been singled and the sema-phores removed and replaced by ugly colour lights, although one of the burned-off stubs can be seen just to the right of the relay box. BR Class '4' 2-6-4T No 80080 approaches with the returning Skegness-Nottingham 'Jolly Fisherman' steam special. *G. W. Morrison/RKH*

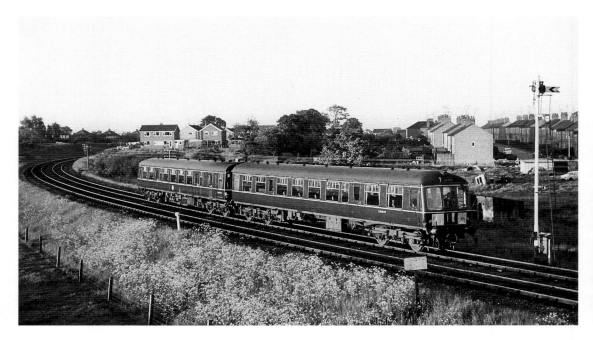

SLEAFORD WEST: On 28 May 1966 the 8.13 pm Lincoln-Sleaford Heavyweight DMU rounds the loop from Sleaford North towards the station. It is approaching Sleaford West where it will join the line from Grantham.

Owing to vegetation, exactly the same viewpoint is not possible today, but a slightly more head-on angle on 1 July 1995 shows the same Sleaford West Distant signal, with the 1333 Peterborough-Doncaster Class 153 disappearing towards the North junction. *Michael Mensing/RKH*

CRANWELL is one of the most historic of Lincolnshire's well-known RAF bases, and was the only one to be served by its own railway, a 5¼-mile branch from Sleaford West, built under the supervision of the GN and opened in 1916. It carried regular passenger traffic until 1927 and freight until 1956. Although never part of BR, it occasionally saw through trains and one of these, a Coronation special, is seen at Cranwell station in 1953, headed by 'J6' No 64196 with another engine at the far end. The gentleman standing on the right is Air Commodore Eeles, the then Commandant of the Base.

Very little trace of the railway at Cranwell remains today, although the station building (just out of shot to the left of the 'past' picture and visible above the row of garages in the 'present' view) is still in use as the main Guardroom. Reference has been made in the Introduction to the generous hospitality afforded to the author and his wife by Flying Officer King and the Cranwell College authorities and a copy of this book is to be placed in the College Library. *RAF Cranwell College Library (S. Squires Collection)/RKH*

RAUCEBY is on the former GN Grantham-Sleaford line, and on 10 July 1965 a Class 25 approaches with a Nottingham-Skegness train. Much of the Great Northern atmosphere remains on 10 April 1993 as No 80080 passes with the outward working of the 'Jolly Fisherman' railtour (see also page 126). The crossing gates are still hand-operated and the demolition of the platform building has revealed the original wooden GN station nameboard, examples of which also survive in this area at Ancaster and Heckington. *J. Spencer Gilks/RKH*

Joint lines and branches to Spalding and Stamford

SPALDING (1): The GN was the first railway to reach Spalding with its Peterborough-Boston-Lincoln line in 1848. By the end of the century, Spalding was an important junction, with services to Sleaford and March over the GN&GE Joint and to the Midlands and East Anglia over the Midland & Great Northern Joint. In this mid-1950s view of the south end of the station 'J6' No 64260 waits at platform 4 with an M&GN line local, and LMS Class '4' 2-6-0 No 43065 stands at platform 5.

The only rail service to Spalding in 1995 is via the GN&GE Joint north to Sleaford and the GN south to Peterborough. The M&GN Joint was completely closed by 1965, the GN to Boston went in October 1970 and the March line in 1982. Only two platforms now remain in use and the remainder are derelict and overgrown. The station nameboard posts remain pointing skywards in May 1995. *N. E. Stead Collection/John Hillier*

SPALDING (2): In this wider view of the south end of the station, we see 'J6' No 64191 acting as pilot on 22 September 1958. A 'B1' stands at platform 1, probably with a Grimsby-Peterborough train.

The footbridge from which the 1958 picture was taken has been demolished, but a similar view is obtainable from the signal box. The contraction of Spalding's railways is well illustrated in this 6 May 1995 view of Class 47 No 47744 departing with a Flower Festival excursion returning to Morpeth via Peterborough. *John Foreman/John Hillier*

SPALDING (3): The famous Spalding Flower Festival takes place annually in early May and today still generates a handful of loco-hauled specials. By contrast, every available siding to the north of the station was occupied on 10 May 1980 with (from left to right) No 47111 from Bristol, No 47412 from King's Cross, No 08133 with stock from Swansea, No 47072 from Oxford, No 47566 from Portsmouth and No 37035 from Wokingham.

Proof that it is not always necessary to go back 30 years or more in order to show dramatic change in our railways is afforded by this view from the same footbridge just 15 years later. The transformation speaks for itself as a Peterborough-Lincoln Class 153 passes an empty unit travelling south on 20 July 1995. The empty and derelict sidings reveal the trackbed of the former GN line north to Boston. *G. B. Wise/RKH*

LITTLEWORTH: No D1791 (later Class 47 No 47310) heads an up coal train through the closed station at Littleworth on the former GN Spalding-Peterborough section on 28 September 1965.

This section was closed to regular passenger traffic in October 1970 along with the remainder of the East Lincs line to Grimsby, but after much protest and a hefty local authority subsidy, it re-opened on 7 June 1971. A Class 153 heads for Spalding on 6 May 1995. *Michael Mensing/John Hillier*

POSTLAND, on the former GN&GE Joint Spalding-March line, was also photographed on 28 September 1965, with No D5655 (later Class 31 No 31229) passing the closed station with an up freight.

The Spalding-March line closed in November 1982. The track was not lifted immediately but was left in place in the hope of a resurgence in traffic, but this did not materialise and lifting started in 1985. In May 1995 the station house survives in private ownership and, behind the photographer, the signal box is virtually intact. The goods yard also contains a collection of wagon bodies, still giving the impression of an operational railway in this remote location. *Michael Mensing/John Hillier*

CASTLE BYTHAM: The western section of the M&GN passed through Lincolnshire from Sutton Bridge (see 'British Railways Past and Present' No 12, East Anglia) in the east and Castle Bytham in the west, near where it joined end-on with the Midland proper. Here is Castle Bytham on 5 August 1957 with Class '4' No 43059 departing with the 9.55 am Saxby-Kings Lynn train.

M&GN passenger services ceased on 28 February 1959, but apart from the removal of the track and fencing the view from the same road bridge in April 1995 is largely unchanged. *Michael Mensing/John Hillier*

NEAR CASTLE BYTHAM: East of Castle Bytham the M&GN crossed the East Coast Main Line on a flyover to the north of Little Bytham station, seen on 8 November 1958 with Class '4' No 43085.

Nothing now remains of the flyover, although much of the fencing is still in situ and the landowner (a steam enthusiast) has left the M&GN trackbed undisturbed so as to let nature take its course. In April 1995 a north-bound Class 158 passes on the ECML. *J. Spencer Gilks/John Hillier*

BOURNE (1): The first railway to reach the pleasant market town of Bourne was the GN branch from Essendine, opened in 1860. The lines east to Spalding and north to Sleaford followed in 1866 and 1872 respectively, and with the opening of the M&GN west to Saxby in 1894, Bourne became a true railway crossroads. The booking hall and station master's house was one of the most interesting railway buildings, and possibly the oldest, in the country. The Red Hall is a Tudor mansion, reputed to have links with Guy Fawkes and the Gunpowder Plot, and the station was built around it. The Hall is on the right in this 1958 picture of a grimy Class '4' leaving the station with an eastbound M&GN local.

The listed Red Hall has been superbly restored in the care of Bourne United Charities and is now used as offices, with lawns covering the former trackbed. The platform areas are now also part of the gardens and the trees forced a slightly different viewpoint for the 1995 picture. *Grimsby Public Library/John Hillier*

BOURNE (2): No 64196 stands alongside the impressive goods shed with a freight from Sleaford on 8 October 1949.

The closure of Bourne's railways started in June 1951 when the Essendine branch became the first line in Lincolnshire to be axed by BR. Passenger services to Sleaford and on the M&GN ceased in 1930 and 1959 respectively and with the end of local freight services in April 1965, Bourne was erased from the railway map. The goods shed remains today in industrial use. *P. H. Wells/John Hillier*

BILLINGBOROUGH & HORBLING station, looking north, probably between 1956 and 1959, with a 'J6' and the local pick-up. This line was finally abandoned in April 1965.

With the exception of the down platform building and signal box, the station is intact today in the ownership of Grimer's Transport Ltd, whose trailers are seen occupying the trackbed in May 1995. With thanks to Mr Grimer Snr for allowing access and for providing the author and his wife with a most entertaining tour of his premises. *N. E. Stead collection/RKH*

TWENTY: Heading back along the M&GN towards Spalding, much of the line ran through flat featureless fenland, and the three intermediate stations served only a smattering of hamlets. Here is Twenty in the late 1950s, with 'J6' No 64172 heading east. The station house and the remains of the westbound platform are seen in the second view in June 1995. *N. E. Stead collection/RKH*

GEDNEY, on the M&GN east of Spalding, is seen on 31 August 1958 as No 43085 leaves with the 10.53 am (Sundays only) Spalding-Hunstanton train. The comparative view in June 1993 shows that the station area is occupied by a haulage contractor, and at the far end one of the GN-style station nameboards survives. *Hugh Ballantyne/RKH*

TYDD: The section of the M&GN to Wisbech and Peterborough branched south at Sutton Bridge and left Lincolnshire at Tydd. On 31 August 1958 Class '4' No 43088 arrives from the south with the 9.55 am (Sundays only) Murrow East-Hunstanton. The up platform and station house survive in June 1995. *Hugh Ballantyne/RKH*

THURLBY was one of the two intermediate stations on the Essendine-Bourne branch, and in this evocative scene on 5 June 1951 is Class '4' No 43061 approaching with the 9.35 am train to Essendine. The branch closed 11 days later. The platform now forms part of a council depot and little else remains to indicate that a railway once ran here. *Mike Black/John Hillier*

BRACEBOROUGH SPA: The other intermediate station on the Bourne-Essendine branch was the single platform at Braceborough Spa, where Class '4' No 43082 calls with the afternoon train from Bourne on 7 April 1951. No doubt it was hoped that the waters of Braceborough would become as famous as those of Bath or Cheltenham, but it was not to be.

In the spring of 1995 the station house has been renovated and is named 'Spa Halt', but the crossing gates and marvellous lamps are no more. *P. H. Wells/John Hillier*

STAMFORD EAST (1):The Midland was the first railway to reach the historic coaching town of Stamford in 1846/48, with Town station on its Syston-Peterborough line. Denied access to Town, the Stamford & Essendine Railway (later part of the GN) opened Stamford East in 1856 as the terminus of its branch from the main line at Essendine, and from 1867 of its line from Wansford. Here is Stamford East on 24 June 1958 with 'N5' No 69262 heading the Essendine branch freight.

Little remains of Stamford East from this viewpoint, although the goods shed on the left has been incorporated into the sheltered housing complex that now occupies the site. The original terminus building survives behind the flats in the centre of the picture. *R. C. Riley/John Hillier*

STAMFORD EAST (2): On 14 April 1957 immaculate 'C12' No 67357 brings the REC 'Charnwood Forester' railtour off the Essendine branch across the connection on to the Midland line at Stamford Junction. The GN box and Stamford East line are on the far side, Stamford shed is in the right background and the Midland box and line to Peterborough on the right. The elegant 'C12s' were associated with the Stamford area for more than 30 years.

A Cambridge-Birmingham Class 158 passes the same location on 9 July 1995. The base of the Midland box can be found amongst the undergrowth on the right. *P. H. Wells/John Hillier*

STAMFORD TOWN (1) looking west on 31 May 1958, with ex-London, Tilbury & Southend 'Atlantic' tank No 41975 arriving with the branch service from Seaton.
  On 8 July 1995 the 1037 Birmingham-Cambridge Class 158 passes the former West signal box (seen in the left distance in the 'past' view), which has been moved to its present location and restored by railway book dealer Robert Humm, whose premises now occupy part of the buildings on the up platform. *R. C. Riley/John Hillier*

STAMFORD TOWN (2): East station closed in 1957, and for the last two years of their life the Essendine branch trains used Stamford Town. Here is the ornate Town station looking east on 31 May 1958, with the branch train headed by 'C12' No 67394.

The same viewpoint 37 years on shows little change apart from the relocated signal box. The 1455 Cambridge-Birmingham Class 158 arrives at platform 2 on 9 July 1995. *R. C. Riley/John Hillier*

Grantham and the East Coast Main Line

CORBY GLEN: Gresley 'V2' 2-6-2 No 60849 rushes through Corby Glen on 5 August 1957 with a southbound express. There is little evidence today that there was once a station at this location. Only the distant buildings, the remains of the bridge abutments and the goods dock on the right provide visible reminders as a southbound HST passes on the slow line in April 1995. *Michael Mensing/John Hillier*

STOKE TUNNEL: The section of the ECML between Grantham and Stoke Tunnel has always been popular with photographers. One of the least-photographed of the 'A4s', No 60018 *Sparrow Hawk,* **heads an up Newcastle express towards the tunnel on 18 April 1955. In the same location exactly 40 years later a southbound IC225 approaches the tunnel.** *Les Perrin/John Hillier*

HIGH DYKE BRANCH (1): This part of the country was rich in ironstone and in 1915 a branch was opened from the ECML at High Dyke to serve the quarries at Stainby and Colsterworth, which supplied steelworks all over the country. On 27 March 1964 No D5652 (later Class 31 No 31226) gently brings loaded iron ore tipplers down the steep gradient just prior to joining the main line (the exchange sidings are visible in the left background of the previous 'past' view).

The modern steel industry imports the bulk of its iron ore and the High Dyke branch closed in August 1973. Here is the view of the cutting in March 1995. *Michael Mensing/CV*

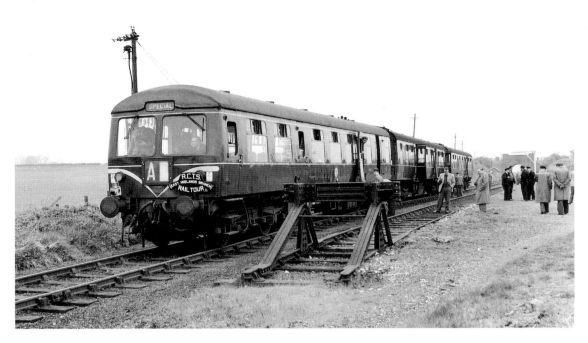

HIGH DYKE BRANCH (2): The iron ore branch sidings at Stainby were visited on 29 April 1961 by a three-car Cravens DMU forming the RCTS 'Vale of Belvoir' railtour. The road bridge remains in March 1995 to identify the now derelict location. *Hugh Ballantyne/CV*

HIGH DYKE SIDINGS: Back on the main line, 'Deltic' No D9012 *Crepello* roars past High Dyke sidings on the climb from Grantham with the 12.20 Hull-King's Cross train on 16 September 1961. The engine is brand new and in original livery, without the yellow front warning panels. The 1254 York-King's Cross IC225 is seen at the same much-rationalised location on 25 June 1995. *Hugh Ballantyne/John Hillier*

GRANTHAM (1): At the north end of Grantham station on 27 September 1953 ex-GN 'Atlantics' Nos 990 *Henry* *Oakley* **and 251 run in with the Doncaster-King's Cross 'Plant Centenarian' special.**

   Grantham station was remodelled as part of the East Coast electrification, and on 25 June 1995 the 1440 Leeds-King's Cross IC225 arrives at the up main platform. *J. F. Oxley/John Hillier*

GRANTHAM (2): 'A4' No 60008 *Dwight D. Eisenhower* heads an up fitted freight through Grantham in 1960. The 'A4s' frequently worked express freights, but evidently the young enthusiast had not seen one doing so before.

Despite the remodelling, much of the old order at Grantham station is still recognisable as a southbound IC225 stands at platform 1 in early 1995. *Les Perrin/John Hillier*

GRANTHAM MPD (coded 35B and later 34F by BR) was adjacent to the station and was an important ECML depot, many expresses changing engines at Grantham. Here is the shed yard looking south on 3 August 1963 with, from left to right, 'B1' No 61392 and a sister, 'A3' No 60048 *Doncaster* and three 'WDs', the right-hand of which is No 90032.

By June 1995 only the distinctive background trees remain to connect the desolate wasteland with the once-busy yard. Even the pony seems fed up with the quality of grazing on offer. *Hugh Ballantyne/John Hillier*

INDEX OF LOCATIONS